GOBLINS AND TROLLS

by John Hamilton

Visit us at

WWW.ABDOPUB.COM

Published by ABDO Publishing Company, 4940 Viking Drive, Suite 622, Edina, Minnesota 55435.
Copyright ©2005 by Abdo Consulting Group, Inc. International copyrights reserved in all countries.
No part of this book may be reproduced in any form without written permission from the publisher.
ABDO & Daughters™ is a trademark and logo of ABDO Publishing Company.

Printed in the United States.

Editor: Paul Joseph
Graphic Design: John Hamilton
Cover Design: TDI
Cover Illustration: *Long Shot Louie* ©1996 Don Maitz
Interior Photos and Illustrations: p 1 *Rumplestiltskin* ©1982 Don Maitz; p 5 *Long Shot Louie* ©1996
Don Maitz; pp 6-7 *Blind Corner* ©1982 Janny Wurts; p 8 *Schneeble* ©1995 Don Maitz; p 9 *Space
Opera* ©1978 Don Maitz; p 10 *Grand Phooba Schnee* ©1995 Don Maitz; p 11 Green Goblin, courtesy
Columbia Pictures; p 12 J.R.R. Tolkien, courtesy Houghton Mifflin; p 13 *The Perils* ©1984 Don Maitz;
p 14 (top & bottom) orcs, courtesy New Line Cinema; p 15 (top) *The Lord of the Rings* book cover,
courtesy Houghton Mifflin; p 15 (bottom) Warcraft III orc, courtesy Blizzard Entertainment; p 16 Orc
(Uruk-Hai), courtesy New Line Cinema; p 17 The Hobbit book cover, courtesy Ballantine Books; p 18
wooden troll sculpture, Corbis; p 19 *Summons Spell* ©1995 Don Maitz; p 20 Peer Gynt and the Troll
King, Mary Evans Picture Library; p 21 troll silhouette, Corbis; p 22 troll chasing moose, Mary Evans
Picture Library; p 23 troll dance, Mary Evans Picture Library; p 24 standing stone, Corbis; p 25 *Bad
Odds* ©1976 Don Maitz; p 26 one-eyed troll, Mary Evans Picture Library; p 28 troll & frog, Mary Evans
Picture Library; p 29 Japanese goblins, Corbis.

Library of Congress Cataloging-in-Publication Data

Hamilton, John, 1959–
    Goblins & trolls / John Hamilton
        p. cm. — (Fantasy & folklore)
    ISBN 1-59197-713-4
    1. Trolls. 2. Goblins. I. Title: Goblins and trolls. II. Title.

GR555.H26 2005
398'.45—dc22

2004046295

CONTENTS

GOBLINS

"Never mess with Goblins, Harry."—Rubeus Hagrid, **Harry Potter and the Sorcerer's Stone.**

 oblins are vile, nasty little creatures, human in shape but much smaller in size. They stand about the height of a table, or shorter. They often have hideous, deformed faces, with wicked red eyes.

Goblins are similar to the brownies of Celtic myths. Like brownies, they sometimes perform household chores, such as sweeping floors or churning milk. But these household spirits are also notorious mischief makers. If their host families anger them, goblins take great pleasure in tipping over pails of milk, or blowing soot down chimneys.

Goblins were originally a part of French folklore. As French folk tales spread to other parts of Europe, stories of goblins spread also. Goblins became more sinister as the stories were told and retold. Today we think of goblins as small, grotesque, and mean-spirited creatures.

Tradition says that goblins first appeared from a cleft, or split, in the Pyrenees Mountains of southwestern France, which is the dividing mountain range between France and Spain. From their mountain home, goblins spread rapidly throughout France, then all over Europe. After infesting Scandinavia, goblins stole aboard Viking raiding ships and came to the British Isles.

The native Druid people of Britain called the invaders *Robin Goblin,* or *robgoblin.* These creatures were later named *hobgoblins.* Hobgoblins as we know them today are actually more helpful than regular goblins. Hobgoblins can pull spiteful pranks, but are mostly helpful to humans, just like their brownie cousins.

True goblins, unlike hobgoblins, are definitely not as friendly as brownies. Their tricks can do serious harm to people.

Far right: Fantasy illustrator Don Maitz's *Long Shot Louie.*

Goblins have been the inspiration for many other characters in books and movies. The author J.R.R. Tolkien created a new form of goblin called *orcs*. The goblins of European folklore weren't formidable enough for Tolkien's books, so he made them even more evil. Still, orcs have definite goblin roots. In Tolkien's stories, *orc* and *goblin* are different names for the same creature.

Trolls are also distant relations to goblins. Trolls are seen in the myths and folklore of many cultures. They come in different shapes and sizes, but they resemble goblins in attitude. Goblins, orcs, and trolls are all monsters of folklore that we humans love to hate.

Right: Fantasy illustrator Janny Wurts's *Blind Corner.*

7

GOBLIN TRAITS

 oblins have a terrible attitude, and it shows in their repulsive faces, especially when they smile. Author Michael Page describes goblins as mischievous to the point of evil. "Like other earth spirits they have human form, but no human ever wore expressions of such malicious mischief and depraved cunning. A goblin smile curdles the blood; a goblin laugh causes milk to sour and fruit to fall from the trees. Even a witch will not allow a goblin at her fireside. She has no fear of it but it is always such a meddling nuisance."

Far right: Don Maitz's *Space Opera.* *Below: Schneeble,* by Don Maitz.

Goblins prefer living in mossy holes, under piles of rocks, or sheltered under the roots of very old trees, especially oaks. Sometimes they take up residence in human homes, where they delight in playing tricks and making noises at night. Some people think their homes are haunted by poltergeists, or ghosts, when actually it is the mischief of goblins that is causing so much commotion.

Goblins enjoy tormenting farm animals, especially horses. Farms that are infested with goblins have a terrible time with horses being run into a lather in the middle of the night. If you see a horse snorting and stamping its feet, or rolling on the ground, it is likely the poor animal has a goblin on its back.

One curious fact about goblins is that they are actually fond of nice children. Goblins will go out of their way to do favors or chores for kind children, or will bring small gifts for well-behaved kids. On the other hand, if children are naughty, goblins can be mischievous or even cruel. They are especially good at hiding under beds, or in closets, and popping out at night to scare and torment children who misbehave.

There is one trick for ridding a house that is plagued with goblins. For some reason known only to goblins, these harmful creatures are attracted to flax seed. If you spread a large handful of flax seed over the floors of your house, the goblins will feel compelled to pick up and count every last seed. Usually there is so much seed the goblins cannot complete the task before the sun rises, when they must retreat to their hiding places. If you repeat this procedure a few times, the goblins will get so bored from picking up and counting the flax seed that they will finally get fed up and leave for good.

Far left: Don Maitz's *Grand Phooba Schnee.*
Below left: The Green Goblin from the movie *Spider-Man.*

ORCS

Orcs are familiar villains to anyone who has read the fantasy books of J.R.R. Tolkien, such as *The Hobbit,* or *The Lord of the Rings.* In Tolkien's stories, orcs are common bad-guy characters. They are a challenging foe for the heroes to battle, yet they are not *too* difficult to defeat. Orcs are dangerous and wicked. They serve the forces of evil. In *The Lord of the Rings*, orcs obey the main villain Sauron, the Dark Lord of the books.

Orcs are almost entirely an invention of Tolkien. It's easy to think of them as very ill-tempered goblins. In fact, Tolkien was thinking of goblins when he came up with his orcs. Most of the author's characters and creatures are based on the established myths and folklore of medieval Europe. These included wizards, warriors, elves, dwarfs, and other familiar characters. But Tolkien had a problem. He needed an enemy for which the audience would feel no sympathy, but who would be formidable enough to be a real challenge for his heroes. With hordes of creatures like these to slay, Tolkien's heroes would seem braver, and his main villains would seem more frightening.

Left: J.R.R. Tolkien, author of *The Lord of the Rings* and *The Hobbit.*
Far right: Don Maitz's *The Perils.*

European folklore didn't really provide anything that fit Tolkien's purposes. *The Lord of the Rings* includes several fierce and gigantic creatures, but you can't have your heroes battling Nazguls or Balrogs in every scene or it would get quite boring. On the other hand, fairies and tommyknockers aren't exactly ferocious. They're more mischief-makers than evil opponents.

Tolkien finally settled on a new form of goblin and renamed them *orcs*. The goblins of European folklore weren't formidable enough for Tolkien, so he beefed them up, made them bigger, more dangerous, more evil. Still, orcs have definite goblin roots. In Tolkien's books, *orc* and *goblin* are different names for the same kind of creature. In his earlier writings, Tolkien wanted to use a name that people were more familiar with. Especially in *The Hobbit*, which Tolkien thought of as a children's book, orcs are sometimes called goblins, and vice versa.

Above and below right: Orcs from Peter Jackson's *The Lord of the Rings: The Two Towers.*

The Lord of the Rings, however, is an adult-themed work. Tolkien wanted to step away from the storybooks, and so goblins gave way completely to the writer's new creation, the orcs. Tolkien didn't want readers to associate fairy tale creatures with his characters, which had different purposes than what is found in folklore. Other races transformed as well, including the elvish Noldor, which are based on the gnomes of European folklore.

In Old English, the word *orc* means "demon." *Orc* had been used in folklore before Tolkien created his fantasies. However, these were usually sea creatures, often serpents, that preyed on whales or unlucky sailors. Tolkien liked the way the word sounded, and used *orc* for his evil brand of goblin.

Tolkien was a soldier who fought for Great Britain during World War I. This experience likely influenced the themes that can be found in his fiction. Tolkien sometimes wrote of how his new race of goblin-like creatures represented the evil and small-mindedness that is often found in human beings.

Surprisingly, Tolkien seldom gave descriptions of orcs in his books. What we do know is that orcs prefer living underground, inhabiting dark places such as tunnels and caves. They are especially numerous in the Misty Mountains and the Gray Mountains of Middle Earth.

Orcs are often described as having sharp teeth, slanting eyes, and broad faces. They are usually misshapen, bent over, and twisted in appearance. Orcs can only come out at night because they hate the sunlight. They often battle dwarfs and other cave-dwelling races, but they are especially hostile toward elves. Orcish food is extremely distasteful to other races. Orcs have been known to eat horses and donkeys, and sometimes even the flesh of humans.

Left: An orc from the video game *Warcraft III.*

Right: The evil wizard Saruman, played by actor Christopher Lee, creates a more destructive orc called an Uruk-Hai in *The Lord of the Rings: The Two Towers.*

One variation of the orc is the dreaded Uruk-Hai. These are an especially vicious type of orc. They are larger and stronger, and can tolerate the sunlight. They were created by the evil wizard Saruman. In *The Lord of the Rings*, the Ent creature called Treebeard says, "It is a mark of evil things that came in the Great Darkness that they cannot abide the Sun, but Saruman's Orcs can endure it, even if they hate it. I wonder what he has done? Are they Men he has ruined, or has he blended the races of Orcs and Men? That would be a black evil."

By creating orcs, J.R.R. Tolkien fashioned an enduring fantasy villain. Orcs are minions of evil that both fascinate and frighten us. With legions of these terrible creatures running loose, there is never a dull moment in the tales of Middle Earth.

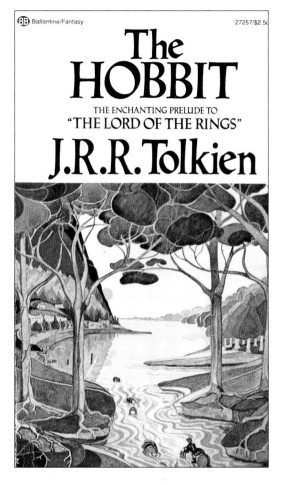

ORCS IN *THE HOBBIT*

In J.R.R. Tolkien's *The Hobbit*, the little hobbit Bilbo and his dwarf companions are captured by a group of goblins, or orcs, who drag them in chains through the tunnels of their mountain home. Finally they meet the leader of the villains, the Great Goblin.

"There in the shadows on a large flat stone sat a tremendous goblin with a huge head, and armed goblins were standing around him carrying the axes and the bent swords that they use. Now goblins are cruel, wicked, and bad-hearted. They make no beautiful things, but they make many clever ones. They can tunnel and mine as well as any but the most skilled dwarves, when they take the trouble, though they are usually untidy and dirty. Hammers, axes, swords, daggers, pickaxes, tongs, and also instruments of torture, they make very well…. It is not unlikely that they invented some of the machines that have since troubled the world, especially the ingenious devices for killing large numbers of people at once, for wheels and engines and explosions always delighted them…. They did not hate dwarves especially, no more than they hated everybody and everything, and particularly the orderly and prosperous…. And anyway goblins don't care who they catch, as long as it is done smart and secret, and the prisoners are not able to defend themselves."

TROLLS

Trolls are huge, ugly, man-like giants or ogres who live mainly in the mountains or deep forests. Some trolls have magical abilities. Most are dim-witted, and can often be outsmarted by clever humans.

There are many parts of the world that have troll-like monsters in their folklore, but they are found most often in the tales and myths of Scandinavia. In Scandinavia, trolls are also called *Trold* or *Trolld*. Thor, the Norse god of thunder and war, hated giants and trolls. He was often away doing battle with these beasts.

Although trolls are usually described as huge in size, in some regions of Scandinavia they are smaller, almost dwarf-like. There is much variation in troll descriptions, depending on where the tales are told. For example, in Ebeltoft, Denmark, trolls are man-eating ogres with humps on their backs who wear pointed red caps. But not far away, in Gudmanstrup, Denmark, the local folklore tells of giant trolls who wear long black clothes.

Right: A wooden sculpture of a happy troll in Norway. Far right: Don Maitz's Summons Spell.

Trolls usually hate people, and sometimes will make a snack out of anyone unlucky enough to be caught. In many places in Scandinavia, trolls are said to hide under bridges, waiting to pounce on unwary travelers.

Trolls are a common villain in many pieces of literature. From age-old folklore to the more modern writings of such authors as J.R.R. Tolkien, trolls have captured the imagination of many storytellers over the years. The famous Norwegian playwright Henrik Ibsen used trolls as an important theme in his 1867 drama *Peer Gynt*. The play is based on the adventures of a boastful, lazy rascal from Norwegian folklore.

In Ibsen's story, trolls represent everything that is nasty and ugly in human nature. The Mountain King rules the trolls from a great hall under a craggy Norwegian peak. When Peer Gynt is brought to the hall deep within the mountain, he is forced to choose between developing himself as a human being or becoming a troll. Said the Mountain King to Peer, "Among men under the shining sky/They say... 'Man to yourself be true!' while here, under our mountain roof/We say: 'Troll, to yourself be—enough!'" Peer eventually flees and makes a narrow escape from the troll kingdom.

Left: A silhouette used on a "troll crossing" sign on a Norwegian roadway.
Far left: In this painting by Arthur Rackham, Peer Gynt faces the Troll King and his minions.

In most stories, trolls wander the land only at night. If trolls are caught by the rays of the rising sun, they are instantly turned to stone. In J.R.R. Tolkien's *The Hobbit*, the hobbit Bilbo Baggins and his dwarf companions, while traveling in the woods, are captured by three trolls named William, Bert, and Tom. The trolls plan to eat the unlucky travelers, but Gandolf the wizard tricks the trolls into arguing amongst themselves until just before dawn. The trolls finally decide to stop bickering and eat their captives, but it is too late.

"… For just at that moment the light came over the hill, and there was a mighty twitter in the branches. William never spoke for he stood turned to stone as he stooped; and Bert and Tom were stuck like rocks as they looked at him. And there they stand to this day, all alone, unless the birds perch on them; for trolls, as you probably know, must be underground before dawn, or they go back to the stuff of the mountains they are made of, and never move again. That is what had happened to Bert and Tom and William."

Far right: Peer Gynt and the Dance of the Trolls, by Arthur Rackham.
Below: A moose is chased through a swamp by a Norwegian troll.

In Tolkien's other books, including *The Lord of the Rings*, trolls appear as servants of the evil Sauron, the Dark Lord of Middle Earth. Sauron made the trolls nastier and stronger, with scaly skin as hard as rock. Tolkien created several different types of trolls, including cave-trolls, snow-trolls, and mountain-trolls. They are a formidable foe for the heroes in Tolkien's stories.

TROLL FOLKLORE

 n the folk tales of Norway, trolls are horrible and hairy. Lady trolls, however, are said to be beautiful, with locks of stunning red hair. Norwegian trolls live together in groups under hills in cave-like dwellings called barrows, which long ago served as graves. The trolls transformed the barrows into stately manors, filled with glittering gold and treasure.

Far right: Don Maitz's *Bad Odds.* *Below:* Legends say that some ancient standing stones are the remains of petrified trolls.

Norwegian trolls aren't quite as nasty toward humans as other trolls. In fact, if a human family pleases them, the trolls will reward the humans with riches. On the other hand, if people anger the trolls, the creatures will wreck the humans' cropland, destroy property, or even kidnap sleeping children.

There are several ways to fight trolls. Branches of mistletoe are said to offer protection against Norwegian trolls. Also, trolls hate noise. Ringing church bells can drive even the most stubborn troll out of the neighborhood. Trolls will turn to stone if struck by the sun's rays. There are many huge, standing stones in the north of Norway that are said to be the remains of petrified trolls.

THE TROLLS IN HEDALE WOOD (A NORWEGIAN FOLK TALE)

In the days of old, in the village of Vaage, there was a poor couple who had many children. Two of their sons grew to be teenagers, and often went roaming around the countryside begging for food and money.

One day the two brothers decided to visit the hut of a falconer in the neighboring town of Maela. They knew a shortcut through the woods, and soon set out to see the falconer's birds.

But their shortcut turned out to be a small path that became narrower and narrower the farther along they walked. When the sun finally set, the brothers strayed from the path completely, and soon found themselves lost in the dark forest.

Unable to continue walking, the brothers lit a fire and then made a bed of moss and branches with an axe that they carried with them. A little while after they laid down to sleep, they heard a creature in the woods, something big snuffling and sniffing with its nose. Then they heard a booming voice say, "I smell human blood here!" Heavy footfalls shook the earth, and the brothers then knew that trolls were coming toward their camp.

The oldest brother took the axe and hid in a bush, and just in time. Out of the darkness strode three bloodthirsty trolls, their heads as high as the fir trees. Luckily, the trolls had only one eye between them. Each troll had a hole in his forehead in which to put the eye, and turned and twisted it with his hands. The troll who came first in line had the eye. His two blind companions walked behind, taking hold of the leader to steady themselves.

When the youngest brother saw the trolls, he gave a frightful yell and fled into the woods. The trolls gave chase, striding right past the brother hidden in the bush. As the last troll walked by, the young man popped out of his hiding place and chopped the troll's ankle with his axe. The troll screamed in pain and fell to the ground. The first troll was so startled that he dropped his eye.

Quick as lightning, the older brother snatched up the eye. It was bigger than two pots put together, and when he looked through it, everything became bright and clear as day.

When the trolls realized the boy had stolen their eye, they threatened him will all kinds of evil if he didn't give it back right away. "Give us the eye, little wasp, or we'll turn you to sticks and stones!" they screeched.

The boy was unafraid. "Now I've got three eyes to myself," he said, "and you three have got none. Not only that, two of you now have to carry the third." The boy threatened to chop all their ankles if they didn't leave the two brothers alone, so that the trolls would have to creep along the forest floor like crabs.

The frightened trolls wailed in misery. They begged for mercy, and even offered the brothers bags of silver and gold, if only they could get their eye back. To this, the brothers readily agreed.

The brothers took the treasure, dropped the eye, and then ran off into the woods toward home. The trolls, after groping around on the forest floor, finally found their precious eye. Then they fled to their underground lair, and were never again heard snuffing around after human blood.

Other Troll Tales

any countries have troll stories that are unique to their cultures. In Iceland, trolls are evil giants who have only one eye, like a cyclops. In the Faeroe Islands (northwest of Scotland and halfway between Iceland and Norway), trolls are called Fodden Skemaend, or the Hollow Men. They are feared for their habit of kidnapping people and keeping them for slaves, often for many years.

The folklore of Finland tells of an evil troll called Sjörtroll, who lives in a large lake near the city of Kökar. The troll is kept prisoner by two magical runic stones that have been placed at each end of the lake. On days when storms or fog blanket the area, the magic of the stones is masked. Many residents refuse to fish on the lake on such days, for fear of the troll reaching up and drowning them.

There are even trolls in the folklore of the Inuit people of Greenland and northern Canada. These creatures are similar to the giant, hairy trolls of Scandinavia. In the Inuit stories, however, the trolls have enormous bellies that drag along the ground as they walk. They also have long, daggerlike fingernails. The trolls of the Inuit like to prowl in the uninhabited hill country, waiting for innocent travelers to capture and eat.

Left: A troll with his pet frog greets two long-tailed creatures.

Trolls, as well as goblins, have become the villains of many legends. These spiteful creatures have made the heroes of many stories more heroic. Recently, author J.K. Rowling has brought goblins and trolls to children's literature. In her series of Harry Potter books, young witches and wizards must find ways to outsmart the dim-witted creatures. Rowling's stories have revived the interest in these disgusting beings.

Left: Goblins and trolls from Japanese folklore.

GLOSSARY

BROWNIE

Brownies are household spirits that live mainly in northern England and Scotland. These tiny fairies are usually shaped like humans. Some are naked and shaggy, while others wear ragged brown clothes. Brownies can be very helpful. They perform many tedious chores for people, such as sweeping, grinding grain, or churning butter. In return, human families give the brownies a bowl of cream or a freshly baked loaf of bread. It is considered good luck to have a brownie living in your house.

FOLKLORE

The unwritten traditions, legends, and customs of a culture. Folklore is usually passed down by word of mouth from generation to generation.

GROTESQUE

Something that appears to be bizarre and distorted. Some people think grotesque objects or creatures are ugly, while others think they are merely different or fantastic.

INUIT

The native people of North America who inhabit northern lands from Greenland and eastern Canada to Alaska. They used to be called Eskimos, but Inuit is now the preferred term.

MALICIOUS

A person or deed that is intentionally cruel, mischievous, or harmful. Goblins are often described as being malicious because they can be so mean.

MEDIEVAL

Something from the Middle Ages.

MIDDLE AGES

In European history, a period defined by historians as between 476 A.D. and 1450 A.D.

MISCHIEVOUS
Full of mischief. Mischievous goblins likes to pull pranks or sometimes cruel tricks that do harm or injury.

MYTHOLOGY
The study or collection of myths. Myths are traditional stories collected by a culture. Their authors are almost always unknown. Myths explain the origin of mankind, or of civilizations. They also explain the customs or religions of a people. Myths are often stories that include the deeds of gods and great heroes.

NOTORIOUS
Something that is well known, especially information about something or somebody that is unfavorable, perhaps even scandalous, but is widely believed.

PETRIFIED
A process in geology where a living thing's cells are replaced with minerals. The result is a rigid stone that resembles the original plant or creature.

RUNIC
Something that resembles the runes of the ancient people of northern Europe. Runes are the characters of the alphabet used by early Scandinavian and Germanic people from about 300 A.D. Some runes are said to have magical abilities, especially when carved in stones that are set into the ground.

SCANDINAVIA
A region of northern Europe that includes Norway, Sweden, and Denmark. Iceland, Finland, and the Faeroe Islands are also often considered Scandinavian.

SINISTER
Something evil and wicked, that threatens harm or misfortune.

INDEX